Nine Lives
Coloring Book

Shoshonna Shoap

Be the person your cat thinks you are.

For all the creative,
animal loving people
in the world.

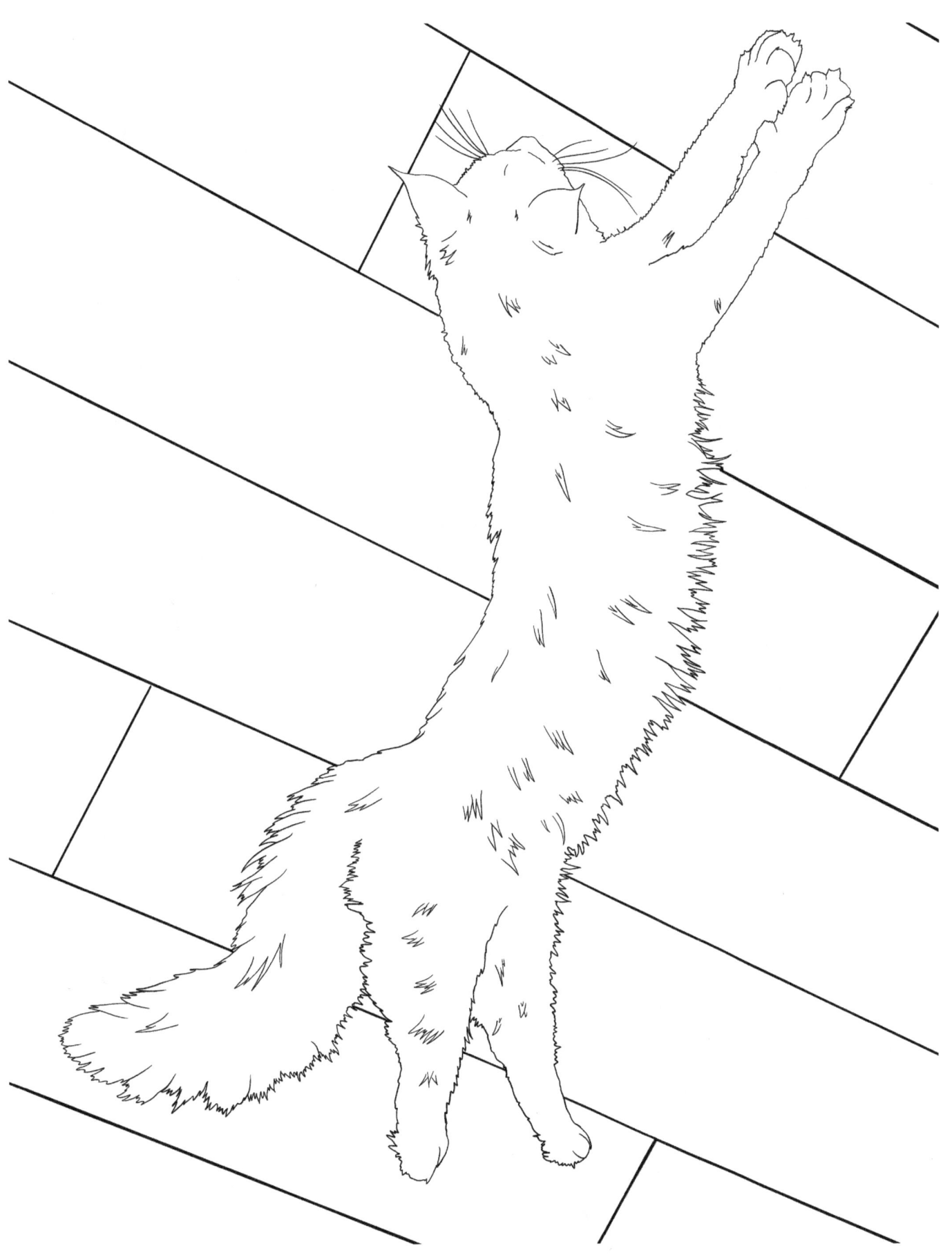

www.ingramcontent.com/pod-product-compliance
Lightning Source LLC
LaVergne TN
LVHW081530060526
838200LV00049B/2275